"Connie Ramsey's book **Pugs are People, Too** is a book about a young girl who has these two adorable pugs named Addie and Charlie who truly believe they are people too. Each adventure they go on is filled with so much fun. You will so enjoy reading this book to your little one, but watch out as I think you just may end up falling in love with these adorable Pug People! I loved this book so much I bought several copies for family members!"

~ Judy O'Beirn, International Bestselling Author of Unwavering Strength series

"**Pugs are People, Too** is a happy and fun story between a girl and her two best friends, Addie and Charlie. Connie Ramsey shows us how much fun we can have in a day with our best friends. A delightful story sure to make you smile and want to play with your furry friends. Friendships truly do come in all shapes and sizes."

~ Jenny Jahnke, author of Lily Finds Hope

"**Pugs are People, Too**, is a delightful peek into the life of two playful pugs. Connie writes brilliantly about the joyful way these two pugs love life and soak up every moment of the day. This is a story that will surely capture your heart."

~ Mickey Eves, Children's Empowerment Coach

"**Pugs are People, Too** is a cute story of puppy love. The way they love life makes us fall in love with them. A dog lovers delight."

~ Colleen Aynn, #1 International Bestselling Author of Sad Sally and the Feeling Friends, www.colleenaynn.com

PUGS ARE PEOPLE, TOO

By
Connie Ramsey

Illustrated by Mickey Eves

Published by
Hasmark Publishing, judy@hasmarkservices.com

Copyright © 2017 Connie Ramsey

Illustration Copyright © 2017 Mickey Eves and Hasmark Services

First Edition

No part of this book may be reproduced or transmitted in any form or by any means, electronic or mechanical, including photocopying, recording or by any information storage and retrieval system, without written permission from the author, except for the inclusion of brief quotations in a review.

Disclaimer

This book is designed to provide information and motivation to our readers. It is sold with the understanding that the publisher is not engaged to render any type of psychological, legal, or any other kind of professional advice. The content of each article is the sole expression and opinion of its author, and not necessarily that of the publisher. No warranties or guarantees are expressed or implied by the publisher's choice to include any of the content in this volume. Neither the publisher nor the individual author(s) shall be liable for any physical, psychological, emotional, financial, or commercial damages, including, but not limited to, special, incidental, consequential or other damages. Our views and rights are the same: You are responsible for your own choices, actions, and results.

Permission should be addressed in writing to Connie Ramsey at www.connieramsey.com or connie@pugsarepeople2.com.

Illustrator, Mickey Eves
mickeyeves1@gmail.com

Cover Design & Book Layout, Anne Karklins
annekarklins@gmail.com

ISBN-13: 978-1-988071-87-9
ISBN-10: 1988071879

*To the big and little people who are captivated with pugs
and all their wacky behaviors and to
my wonderful husband who is always there for me
and is my strongest supporter.*

— CR

My best friends are my pugs, **ADDIE** and **CHARLIE**. They like to do everything I do.

We have lots of fun together. When I play dolls, Addie lets me dress him up with a hat, sunglasses, and jewelry.

At Halloween, Charlie also likes to dress up in a costume. One year he wore a Superman shirt and he became **"SUPER PUG!"**

When it is cold outside, Addie and Charlie wear warm sweaters. When I put boots on Charlie's feet, he runs around in circles until he shakes them off.

Once we get our warm clothes on, we go outside to play in the snow. Charlie jumps onto the sled with me and

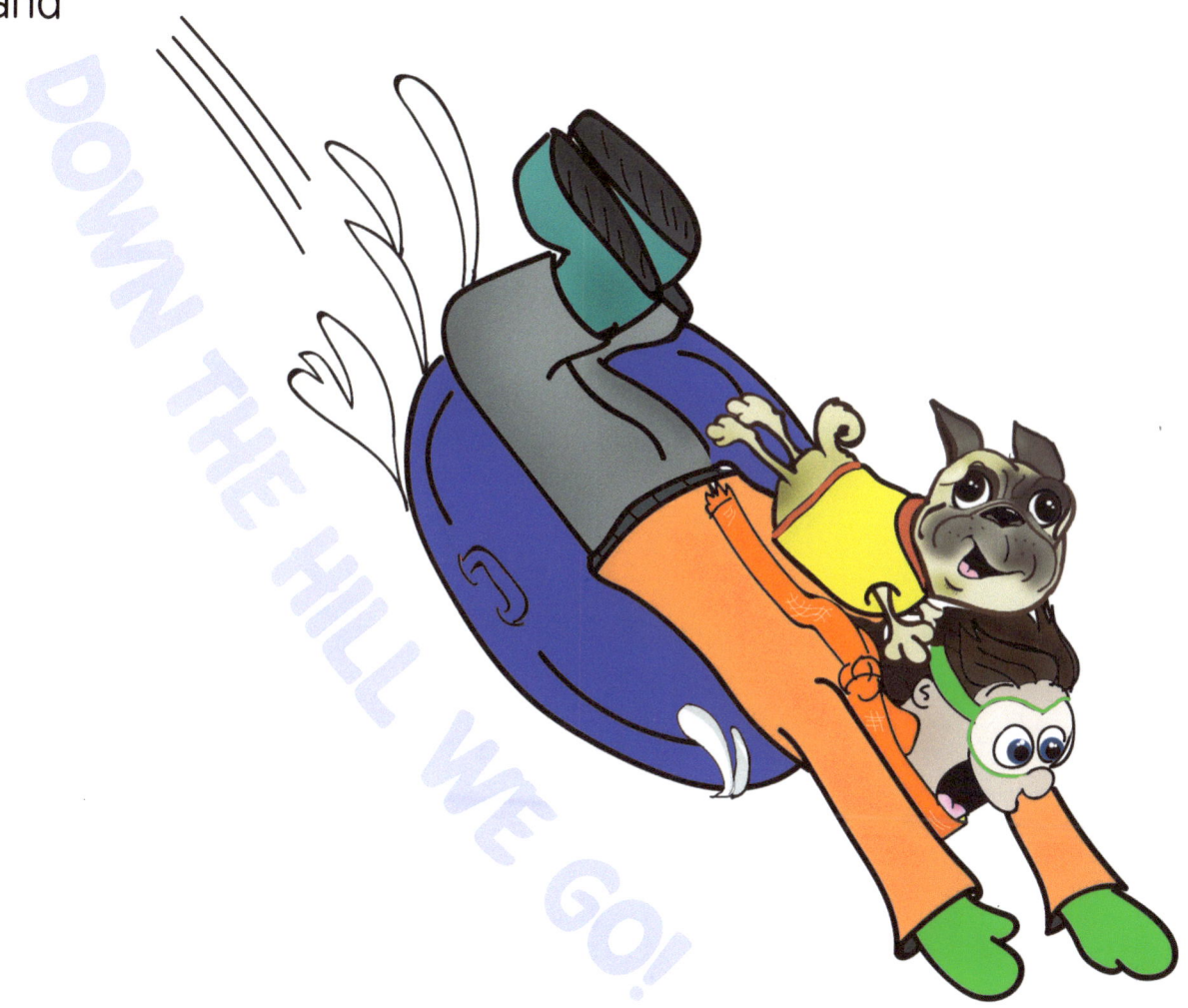

DOWN THE HILL WE GO!

Charlie likes to play in the snow and catch snowflakes on his tongue.

When he's all done playing in the snow, he picks his feet up one at a time, trying to shake the snow off his paws!

When we get tired of playing outside, we go inside to rest on the couch and read a book or watch TV.

Addie and Charlie fall asleep snoring.

When a dog barks on TV, Addie suddenly wakes up. He barks angrily at the TV, trying to protect me from the TV intruder.

When I fall asleep on the couch, Addie suddenly wakes up and wants to play.

He jumps off the couch and grabs my favorite stuffed animal. He runs to show me, hoping I will try to take it away from him. We end up playing tug-of-war until one of us gets tired.

Running and playing with Addie gives me an appetite, so I ask Mommy for a snack.

When I sit at the kitchen table,
Addie jumps up and sits beside me.
He thinks he is a person, too!

After snack, Mommy says it is time to go to the library to renew our books. Addie jumps up barking wildly, because he wants to go with us. He is the first one in the car and he sits in the driver's seat acting like he is going to drive the car.

When Mommy gets into the car, Addie jumps into the back seat to sit beside me. He likes to wear my headphones and listen to my music with me.

As we head home from the library, Mommy says it is time to get ready for bed. Addie and I run into the house, and Addie **BEATS ME UP THE STAIRS.**

Addie runs to my bedroom so he can be the first one in my bed! He likes to snuggle with me during the night.

Mommy comes to my room to read us a story. Addie and I become very sleepy and soon we are sound asleep.

Addie snores, but I am too tired to hear. Mommy kisses us good night, and tells us to sleep tight. We are sound asleep as Mommy turns out the light.

Once Upon a Time ...

GOOD NIGHT, SLEEP TIGHT!

ABOUT THE AUTHOR

Connie Ramsey

Connie grew up in an Air Force family and moved frequently as a young child. She graduated from Duke University with a degree in nursing and enjoyed working in various community organizations. She recently retired after working thirty years as an elementary School Health Nurse. Connie is married to her best friend and soul mate, Tom Ramsey, and they have a blended family of five children, eleven grandchildren, and two grand-dogs who keep them entertained all of the time. Their free time is spent teaching karate and self defense, traveling, and celebrating special occasions with their family.

One of Connie's favorite places to vacation is the coast of Florida along the Gulf of Mexico. She is passionate about assisting the Clearwater Marine Aquarium in their efforts to do Rescue, Rehab, and Release and she recently "adopted" Winter, the dolphin who has an artificial tail: https://seewinter.com/. Her hobbies are hunting seashells along the beach, biking, writing, and reading a good book.

Note to the Readers

Pugs have always been in Connie's family tree from grandparents down to great grandchildren. The pugs won a place in their hearts and participated in all of their family activities. As an elementary school nurse, Connie displayed pug pictures in her office, and the students always wanted to ask questions about the names of the pugs and what they were doing, and then they would share stories about their dogs or pets. Pugs have a way of breaking down barriers and opening conversations even with the shyest person.

It is Connie's hope that this book will create excitement and reading enjoyment in your family and be cherished as a favorite book for years to come.

She loves to hear from her readers and can be contacted at connie@pugsarepeople2.com or through her website www.connieramsey.com.

For more information
and to obtain a free bonus gift, go to Connie's website at
www.connieramsey.com.

The Literary Fairies

we make your literary wish come true

Addie and Charlie

are excited to introduce you to their friends

The Literary Fairies

TLF is a cool place where you can find out
how YOU could become a published author or
how to help grant a literary wish.
Have an adult visit TLF website for more details about
what we do and how you can help, and also get your
FREE colouring pages and "fill-in-the-blank story"

http://theliteraryfairies.com/free-for-kids/

www.ingramcontent.com/pod-product-compliance
Lightning Source LLC
Chambersburg PA
CBHW040032050426
42453CB00002B/88